Old-Time
BANJOCR
5 String Open Back
By Robert Browder w

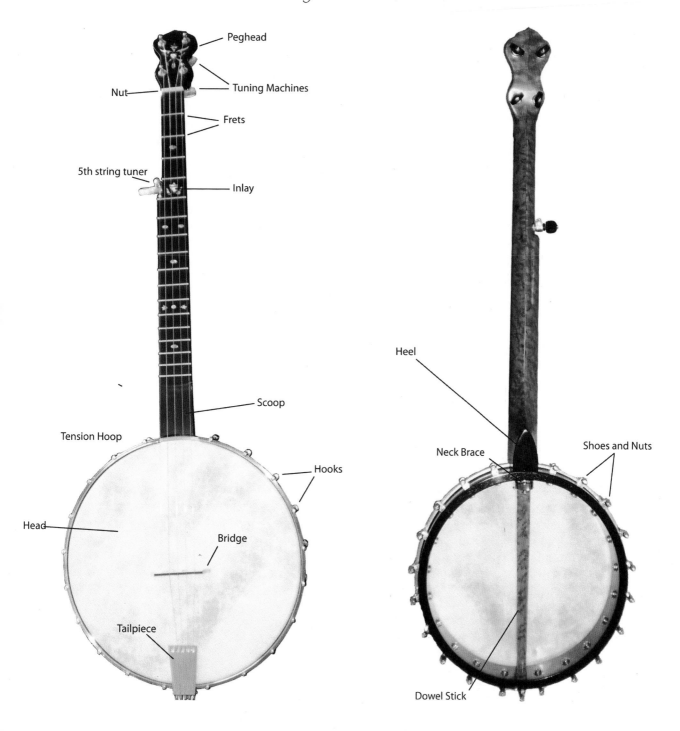

Peghead

Tuning Machines

Nut

Frets

5th string tuner

Inlay

Heel

Scoop

Tension Hoop

Neck Brace

Shoes and Nuts

Hooks

Head

Bridge

Tailpiece

Dowel Stick

ThumpFactor Publishing
P.O. Box 1468
Radford, Virginia 24143

www.banjocraft.com

Design and Layout by Robert Browder

Backcover photo by David Franusich
All other photos by Mac Traynham and Robert Browder

Editing by Jenny Traynham, Mac Traynham, Jennifer Barton, and Robert Browder

ISBN 978-0-615-41075-3

Table of Contents

This book is intended to be accessible to wood workers and banjo people of all stripes and skill levels. If you are completely new to wood working you may wish to consult an introductory manual, tolerant friend, or better yet, get a part time job in a custom cabinet shop. It is important at the beginning to become familiar with safety concerns associated with the operation of power tools as it is possible to become badly injured or even get yourself killed from the misuse of a power tool. The biggest dangers in the wood shop are not paying attention, being careless, and failing to think an operation through.

My own interest in banjo making developed through playing music and the wish to own a really cool banjo. Although having done some very basic woodworking in my past I was poorly equipped for banjo making. I started out by making "cookie tin" banjos in my living room. The "cookie tin" phase helped me to acquire some of the basic hand tools I needed and helped me appreciate the skill that is required to make good use of them. About that time I was fortunate to become acquainted with Mac Traynham who is not only a great banjo maker and player, but also runs a cabinet shop. With lots of patience on my own part and on the part of Mac, I slowly developed the skills required to make a great banjo.

This text focuses on the construction of 5 string open back banjos. Much of the information here is transferable to other types of woodworking and instrument building projects. Hopefully I've broken up the task of making a banjo into smaller tasks that make the whole process easy to understand and easily accessible. There are often many ways to accomplish the same job, the processes here are for reference only. Every shop, tool, and woodworker is a little different so adjust accordingly.

Have Fun!

Early Considerations

Making a banjo has several procedures involved. Most of these procedures have multiple steps. It is a good idea to think about all of the parts and the steps that are required to make them before ever beginning to build a banjo. It is a good idea to plan out your design. There may be some confusing terms here in the beginning. Browsing this manual from cover to cover and allowing yourself to skip between sections will likely prove helpful. It is also beneficial to have a banjo on hand to use as a three dimensional model. Whenever you have the opportunity, take special notice of the structural details of other banjos.

Every banjo has a neck and a rim. The neck allows for noting and the rim acts as a frame to stretch a membrane across. The membrane, which is commonly called the "head", acts as the soundboard. The neck and the rim are constructed separately. Bringing these two basic parts together to become a banjo is a challenge and is accomplished by adding a third basic part, the dowel stick. The dowel is found on the inside of the banjo rim. The dowel is rarely seen while the banjo is being played. In the case of a resonator banjo the dowel is almost never seen because it is concealed by the resonator. The dowel stick is purely functional. The dowel brings the neck and rim together.

Scale length:

The scale length is the length of the string from the nut to the bridge. The scale length of the string also represents the part of the string that vibrates when struck. Many resonator banjos feature a longer scale length. Some old time or open back banjos feature a shorter scale length. Generally, a longer scale length means a longer neck and a greater distance between each fret. The relationship between the length of the string, the gauge or diameter of the string, its weight, and the tension needed to bring it up to pitch are of interest to the builder of most any kind of string instrument. The longer a string is the heavier it will be, thus greater tension is needed to bring it up to pitch. More tension is also required to bring a larger diameter string up to pitch as they are heavier. Greater tension usually results in vibrations of greater amplitude being communicated to the head, often resulting in a louder instrument.

A variety of tunings are employed in open back banjo playing. The scale length should accommodate for this facet of the instrument's intended use. I like 25.5" which is the same scale length as many popular guitars. It is a scale length that allows for tuning up to the high keys without a significant risk of string breakage, but is long enough for the lower keys to sound good without the strings being too loose.

The Rim

A banjo rim, sometimes called the pot, has several functions. It acts as the frame to stretch the head across, acts as the sound chamber, and gives us something to attach the neck to. As with all other aspects of the banjo there is a good deal of variety in rims. The main thing is that it be strong enough to hold tension on the head without a risk of warping. A good banjo rim need not be overly heavy but should act as a counter balance for the neck. If a rim is too light the neck will feel heavy in the noting hand and will have to be supported by that hand. It is better if the banjo balances itself, freeing up the noting hand for noting. The rim, in acting as an anchor for the neck must have some way to accommodate the dowel stick, this is accomplished by the *rim* dowel stick hole. The neck also has a dowel stick hole, so be careful not to get the two terms confused as they will often be mentioned together. The *neck* dowel stick hole and the *rim* dowel stick hole must be coordinated with each other, this takes careful planning. 180 degrees from the *rim* dowel stick hole is the tail of the rim. The tail of the rim has a special hole that accommodates a special screw that is known as the end pin screw. This screw holds the dowel to the rim at this end.

Rim Diameter

Most modern open back banjos have an 11" or 12" rim. The diameter of the rim affects several aspects of a banjo. The size of the rim defines the size of the head. The banjo with the 12" rim often has a bit mellower tone than the banjo with the 11" rim. The 12" banjo often has greater volume potential than the 11" as well. I like both the 11" and 12" rims, but

The square hole seen here is the rim dowel stick hole. The inner laminations of this rim are straight grained maple and the outer most lamination is walnut. The rim cap is also walnut.

lean towards the 12" as my personal favorite. The size of the rim also plays an important role in planning. The neck for a banjo with a 12" rim is slightly shorter than the neck for an 11" rim banjo in the case that they both use the same scale length. The diameter of the rim will also have some affect on the balance and "feel" of the banjo when it is held on one's knee.

Rim Thickness

I have in the past constructed banjo rims from commercially produced drum shells. Using a drum shell for a rim reduces the amount of work involved in building a banjo significantly. It's not a bad solution and makes for a fun instrument that can be enjoyed for many years. Many drum shells measure about 3/8" thick. This is really a little thin and a little light for my own taste. The drum shell being light in weight can make for a banjo that feels neck heavy. I prefer to make a rim from scratch that is 1/2" thick or a little thicker. It looks and feels sturdier and I think the mass of the rim may create some positive tonal qualities as well. The weight of the rim is naturally related to its thickness. The weight of the rim will contribute to the balance and "feel" of the banjo as does the diameter. This "made from scratch" rim is constructed from four thin strips of wood formed and glued together. The process for constructing a rim from scratch is fully detailed in the Rim section.

Rim Depth

The depth of a banjo rim can have significant impact on the tone of the instrument, much as the depth of a drum changes its sound. Depth contributes to the total weight of the rim also. The depth of the rim also plays an important role in the planning of a banjo.

The Neck

The part of the banjo that is commonly called the neck has four main parts, the neck itself, the heel, the fingerboard, and the peghead, each of which have features of their own. The neck itself acts as a handle. The noting hand slides up or down it in order to reach different notes. The shape and size of the neck is important. Strength is a consideration with the neck. The strings will exert constant tension on the neck throughout the life of the banjo. The neck must be strong enough to remain straight. It is a good idea to reinforce the neck. I use a steel bar to reinforce my necks, the details are discussed in the Neck section.

The back of the neck, where the palm and heel of the hand hold or move along it is shaped with the hand in mind. I like a gentle V shape, because it suits my hand nicely and gives the thumb of my noting hand something to push against. The shape of the neck also contributes to the weight of the neck. I like for the neck to be as thin as possible while still providing an ample handle.

The Heel

The heel is the part of the neck that meets the rim. The heel must be strong. The end of the heel that meets the rim will be given a radius that matches the diameter of the rim.

The neck will be mounted to the rim at a slight angle, this means that the mating surface of the heel has both a radius and an angle cut into it. The heel also acts as a place for the dowel stick to mount into and must have a hole drilled into the surface that mates with the rim to accommodate the tenon of the dowel stick. This is a feature that will be addressed the neck section.

The Peghead
The peghead serves as a place for the tuning machines to mount. It too must be strong. The peghead angles back from the plane of the fingerboard. Take some extra consideration of the grain orientation in this area when planning as this tends to be the weakest and most vulnerable part of many stringed instruments.

The Fingerboard
The fingerboard is the front side of the neck and acts as the playing surface for the noting hand. Some banjos are fretted and some have no frets. In either case the fingerboard must be wide enough to accommodate the fingers.

Neck Length:
Here is something to think about: if the rim is 11" or 12" in diameter and the scale length is 25.5" from nut to bridge, how long should the neck be? That depends on where you want the bridge to rest on the head. **A great deal of a banjo's tone and over tones will be determined by where the bridge rests on the head.** I like mine to be almost in the middle, about 5.5" from the tail of the rim in the case of a 12" rim, more like 5" or a little less for an 11" rim. This area is sometimes called the "sweet spot" by makers and players because it sounds so nice about there. So in steps, to figure out the length of the neck...

1. Scale Length
2. Rim Size
3. Bridge Placement
4. Subtract; (Rim Size) - (Distance of bridge from tail) = Distance from bridge to beginning of fingerboard.
5. Subtract; (Scale Length) - (Distance from Bridge to beginning of fingerboard) = length of fingerboard.

Draw some pictures to help yourself figure this out the first time.
With a 25.5" Scale length, my fingerboard for a 12" rim comes out to about 19". And for an 11" rim, about 19.5". Knowing the length of the fingerboard we can now consider the total length of the neck. In addition to the length of the fingerboard the total neck length

This wooden dowel features a round tenon on one end which will eventually be glued into the heel of the neck

also includes the length of the peghead. So, if we add 7" to the fingerboard length to accommodate the length of the peghead that gives a total length of 26.5". For an 11" rim make the neck 1/2" longer.

The Dowel Stick

As noted earlier the dowel stick brings the rim and the neck together. The dowel can take different forms. I use a wooden dowel and spend some time on the details of that later on. Many banjos feature a steel rod that serves as a dowel. Some banjos even have two steel rods that may be adjusted to change the neck angle. In any case the dowel accomplishes its job by mounting to the tail of the banjo rim and by attaching to the neck. In the case of the wooden dowel, the dowel is joined to the neck using a tenon and the neck/dowel is held securely to the rim with a brace. The other end of the dowel is held in place by a screw. In the case of a steel dowel, the dowel screws into the heel of the neck and screws or bolts into the rim at its opposite end.

Location of the Dowel Stick Holes
(Where The Neck Meets the Rim)

The place where the neck and rim meet is really the heart of the banjo. There is a lot that happens in this area. This is where the dowel stick inserts and is glued into the *neck* dowel stick hole to join it to the neck. The dowel then inserts into the *rim* dowel stick hole. The dowel is not glued to the rim. The coordinated location of the dowel stick holes is critical. It is wise to have a target depth in mind for the rim from the very start. This means choosing a tone ring style from the start or at least making a plan that allows for flexibility. I like for the edge of my fingerboards to come out just even with the top of the banjo head. To make this happen it is essential to plan out the placement of the *neck* dowel stick hole and the *rim* dowel stick hole. The total depth of the rim can be found by measuring its depth with the tone-ring in place. As can be seen in the picture at right the dowel joins the neck at a depth which allows for the tension hoop rabbet. The tension hoop must have this space in order to be tightened properly. Most tension hoops need at least a 5/8" deep tension hoop rabbet. A bit deeper is not uncommon. A target depth of 1 1/2" from the face of the fingerboard for the *center* of the *neck* dowel stick hole is okay but should be adjusted for each banjo.

Above right: The tension hoop rabbet

At left: The hole for the neckbrace pin.

Below: The rim's dowel stick hole with the dowel inserted

Wood Selection

There are many suitable woods for building banjos. Among my own personal favorites for the neck and rim are maple, walnut, and cherry. However, some builders choose to use apple, mahogany, sycamore, ash, alder, poplar, hickory, and on and on. I usually prefer to make the fingerboard and accent pieces like the peghead overlay, rim cap, and the heel cap from ebony or rosewood.

The main thing in the choice of banjo wood is that it be strong and not too heavy. Pine, cedar, and spruce are all too light, and probably not strong enough. Oak and locust woods are a bit on the heavy side for my taste, although they are quite strong. The exception I have seen is tack head banjo rims made from one solid piece of bent oak, which seemed like a good solution in that case. There are varying qualities of wood in all species and that is part of what makes wood so fun, every piece is different! I like to use figured woods for their beauty and challenge. To read more about wood, check out <u>Understanding Wood</u> by R. Bruce Hoadley.

Hardware & Parts

There is a good bit of specialized hardware in a banjo and when it comes to vintage and hand crafted banjos there is a good deal of variety. Most of the modern cannot be found in the hardware store and so must be sent away for from various suppliers. It is a good idea to become familiar with the hardware before you begin work on the banjo. It is a good idea to find out the dimensions of the parts that will be fit directly to the wood of the banjo, such as, the tuning machines, the shoe bolts, and the neck brace. Knowing the dimensions of your hardware will help you make your wooden parts correctly. Purchasing some hardware is a sure way to learn their exact dimensions. Following is a detailed list of the usual hardware that is currently widely available through catalogue and online suppliers.

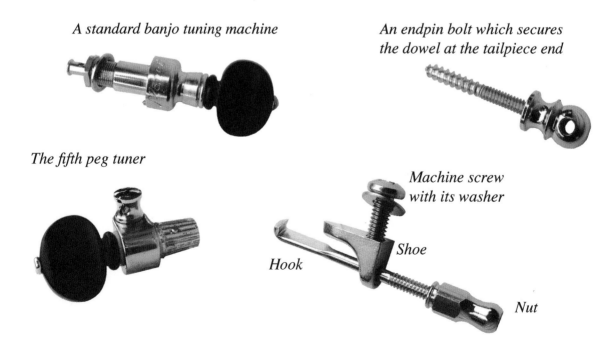

A standard banjo tuning machine

An endpin bolt which secures the dowel at the tailpiece end

The fifth peg tuner

Machine screw with its washer

Shoe

Hook

Nut

Tuning Machines

In ages past the banjo often featured friction pegs, tapered pegs that fit into similarly tapered holes. These can still be found on violins and some gourd banjos made today. They are seldom featured on steel string banjos. With the industrial revolution wooden friction pegs gave way to machined friction pegs, the friction in this case being created by a screw. Later, machined friction pegs gave way to the modern geared machine tuner. Most modern banjos feature geared tuning machines that, unlike guitar tuners, protrude straight back from the peghead. There are a few different makers of modern tuners. There are also tuners available which have the look of a friction peg but are actually cleverly disguised geared tuners. The fifth peg tuner also deserves mention here. It is a special tuner that is pressed into the side of the neck at the place where the fifth string begins. Most of them are geared, but I have seen some that were of the friction type.

The parts of the neck brace.

The plate

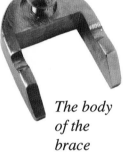

The body of the brace

Hooks, Shoes, Bolts, and other Stuff

Hooks are threaded on one end and feature a hook on the other, they hold the drum part of the banjo together and come in two varieties, round and flat. This distinction refers to the shape of the hook part of the hook. The round hook is used with the notched tension hoop, and the flat hook is used with the grooved tension hoop. It is of course possible to use one for the other but the results are not as good.

The pin

The hooks are one half of a working fixture, the other half is the **nut** which threads onto the hook and holds it onto the shoe and allows for tightening the head. Nuts are available in a variety of sizes and shapes. There are open end nuts and closed end nuts. They play a role in planning because it is nice if the ends of the threaded hooks do not protrude out the back of the nut. Sometimes a hook may have to be cut short so that it does not stick out.

Shoes sometimes called L-shoe brackets are pretty standard. The shoe bolts to the rim, and the hook to the shoe. Most modern shoes have a 12-24 thread size. Some older banjos feature a round shoe, some even feature die-cast shoes in the shapes of animals or other decorative elements. There are considerations to be made when choosing the placement of the shoe on the rim. If the shoe is placed without enough space between its top edge and the bottom of the tension hoop the head will not be able to be fully tightened.

The **Bolts** that fit the shoes are often 12-24 thread size as well, in any case they must match the shoe that they hold on. The bolts that come with the shoes are usually too long for the thickness of my rims. Sometimes I cut them down to size with a saw and smooth down the rough ends on the grinder. More often I order some machine screws that are the right length.

The **Neck Brace** is a great piece of hardware to have and facilitates the use of a wooden dowel. The brace pulls the heel of the neck snuggly against the rim. It also allows the application of additional pressure as the instrument settles. The neck brace consists of four parts, the brace, the screw, a plate, and a pin. The pin mounts into the dowel stick through a small hole drilled just for it, called the *pin hole*. The pin hole need not be an overly tight fit. The location of the pin hole is essential to the operation of the brace. The

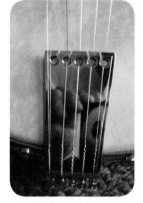

An adjustable angle tailpiece

brace itself straddles the dowel and uses the pin as a fulcrum by which it can pivot and apply pressure. The brace also has a threaded hole for the screw. The screw is tightened to pull the neck snug. The plate sits on top of the brace, between the screw and the rim and gives the blunt end of the screw and the legs of the brace something solid to bear against, preventing it from marring the inside of the rim.

The **End Pin Screw** holds the other end of the dowel stick firmly against the inside of the rim. One end of the screw has wood threads and the other has machine threads and a little brass ball that screws onto it. The little ball has a hole in it to that allows the tailpiece to fasten to it.

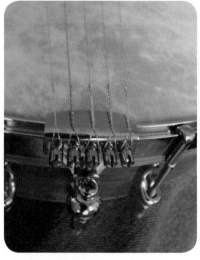

The no-knot tailpiece

Tailpieces

Tailpieces come in a lot of different varieties and they can be divided roughly into two groups: tailpieces which allow for adjustment and those that don't.

The No-Knot tailpiece is perhaps the most common today. It is a favorite with me as it simply offers a way to hook it onto the end pin nut, a plate to keep the strings off the tension hoop, and five little knobs to hook the strings over. Simple and good!

Adjustable Angle tailpieces are nice too. They have a metal plate that protrudes over the banjo head and an adjustment screw, together they create the option of adjusting the angle

A rim with the scalloped secondary tone ring for a Whyte Lady

Top: *The plain rolled brass tone ring.*
Bottom: *The "tube" part of the tone ring for the Tubaphone tone ring.*

of the strings over the bridge. I like these for certain banjos. I think they may have a little less tonal ring than the no-knots. They also offer the chance to "dress up" a banjo a little.

Tension Hoop

The tension hoop holds the head on and gives the hooks something to grab onto. Most tension hoops are made from brass. A lot of them are plated with nickel. There are two basic kinds of tension hoops: grooved and notched. The grooved type has a groove that runs around the top edge of the hoop, flat hooks are used with this type of hoop. The other kind is a notched hoop which has notches for the hooks already cut into it. This means that the number of hooks and their spacing is already defined, so you have to work to that. Round hooks are typically used with the notched hoop. I prefer the grooved hoop. It allows for different hook arrangements and does not poke my arm as much as the notched hoop when playing the banjo. It is also much more forgiving of a shoe bolt hole that is slightly out of place.

Tone Rings

When metal working tools became wide spread in the U.S. in the late 1800's and early 1900's banjo makers went wild with tone ring designs. Brass is usually the metal of choice for tone rings. There are many different kinds of tone rings out there today. I'll touch on just a few of them here. The simplest tone ring is no tone ring. Some banjos feature a beveled edge where the head sits on the rim with no tone ring at all. I have heard some really good sounding old time banjos with this feature.

Rolled Brass is about as plain as a metal tone ring gets. It is simply a piece of round brass rolled into a ring that matches the outside circumference of the rim. I like this type of tone ring very much. It has a great old time sound and may be my favorite. The plain rolled brass tone ring is also the easiest to plan for when building a banjo as it simply sits on the top edge of the rim.

The Little Wonder tone ring is much like the plain brass one, except that it has a spun brass, often nickel plated sleeve that sits over the brass ring. The Little Wonder is a tiny bit louder and brighter than the plain brass ring. It also requires a little more work with the lathe, or possibly the router, as a very small ledge must be cut into the outside of the rim to make room for the sleeve. The idea is to make the sleeve flush with the outside of the rim.

The Whyte Lady tone ring is similar to the Little Wonder in that it features a brass ring trapped by a sleeve. However, the Whyte Lady also incorporates the use of another scalloped ring underneath the round brass ring. The Whyte Lady offers a bright clear tone with a good bit of volume. This tone ring requires a ledge to be cut into the top edge of the rim for the scalloped ring to sit on and a smaller ledge to make the outer sleeve sit flush with the outside of the rim.

The Tubaphone represents the loudest of the tone rings commonly found in open back banjos used for Old-Time and Clawhammer playing styles. It also features the brass rod trapped by a sleeve, only this one sits on top of a hollow tube with holes drilled into it. They're bright and loud! The lathe work for the tuba-phone is similar to the Whyte lady.

Heads

In the olden days animal hides were used for the head. Many players still prefer skin heads, however, I like the synthetic ones. There are several varieties of synthetic or plastic heads on the market today. Following is a brief description of each kind of head.

Natural Animal Hide or Skin is the most authentic head for a banjo. Skin has a great sound with a terrific thump factor. There are however some major draw backs of using a hide head. They are sensitive to humidity fluctuations. In the course of a day, it is likely that you will have to retune your banjo a bit. For some it's worth it. The inside of the head may be varnished to counter act some of the effects of humidity. Goat and calf skin is commercially available through lutherie supply houses.

Synthetic Skin Heads, sometimes known by the trade name "fiber-skyn", are my current favorite. They offer a good bit of the warmth that makes a hide head so appealing without the sensitivity to humidity. They also look like hide on the outside which I like.

Renaissance Heads are alright too, although a little too bright for my own playing. They have a translucent look to them and are pretty loud. I have liked them very much on certain banjos.

Weather King Heads are the original plastic banjo head. You've probably seen them on resonator banjos. Plain white, super bright, some come frosted, some come plain. Often the choice for bluegrass playing, these things could once be seen and heard on the banjo of many an old-timer.

The Neck

One solid piece of wood may be used to make the workpiece that will eventually become the neck. Two pieces may also be glued together to make the dimensions. Depending on the thickness that you begin with, you may also have to add some "ears" to make up the width of the peghead. I like to use two pieces of wood and "book-match" mine because it looks so nice. This practice also gives me the flexibility to use wood of smaller dimensions which is sometimes easier to come by. I also like to accent the glue joint by adding a thin strip of veneer between the two pieces. I detail the two-piece process here as it involves more steps and the one-piece process may be inferred from it with relative ease. After the workpiece is trimmed to suitable starting dimensions the process of making all the various features of the banjo neck begins. Here is a quick run down of the procedures involved. The order of these steps many be adjusted to suit.

1. Workpieces are trued on the jointer
2. Gluing (if two piece neck)
3. The side profile is cut out, then the neck blank is left to cure a while.
4. The neck is reinforced.
5. The ears are added
6. The peghead overlay and fingerboard are added.
7. The neck heel dowel stick hole is drilled.
8. The neck heel radius is cut.
9. The front profile is cut out.
10. Inlay
11. Shaping
12. Fret work

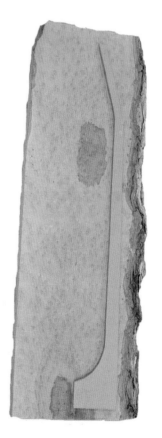

Assessing the potential of a piece of raw lumber using the side profile neck pattern.

First the raw lumber must be dimensioned to the proper sizes. The very minimum dimensions for a neck workpiece whose scale length is to be 25.5" is about 27" long. This figure is developed from our scale length calculations earlier and breaks down like this; the length of the fingerboard plus 6.5 or 7 inches for the peghead. The initial *width* of the workpiece should be equal to the depth of the banjo rim. 3" width is what I begin with. Some of this width will be trimmed away, it is good if the heel of the neck matches the depth of the rim. The *thickness* of the workpiece corresponds to the width of the fingerboard at its widest place. 2" thick is the very minimum acceptable. I like to make my workpiece a little longer, wider, and thicker than the previous measurements just to have a little extra. If you are planning to make more than one banjo it is possible to save material by making a workpiece that you can get two or more necks out of. There are various ways you can "nest" the side profiles of the neck . It is also possible to glue on a piece to make up the dimensions for the heel, this will allow you to "nest" the necks even more closely.

Preparing the Neck Workpiece

1. Choose suitable wood. Take a good long look at your lumber before you begin. Hold it. Tap it. Think it over a little. Look down the length of your board and try to identify any warps or irregularities. Look across the board too see if it has any "cup". Lay the neck pattern on the lumber and look at it. Are there any warped areas, cracks, or knots that fall into the shape of the neck? Plan to leave out the ugly stuff. Also, consider the rim and whether there is enough lumber to make both a rim and a neck. Skipping ahead for a look at the rim section might be advisable here. I typically prefer to make the neck and rim from the same wood. Even from the same board if possible. Start with a board that is at least 1.25" thick in the rough. If it is already surfaced it might be possible to use a board as thin as 1" IF it is VERY straight, but any thinner seems unrealistic for a two piece neck. The thinner the board you start with is, the more important it is that it be straight. With a thicker piece, a warp may be worked out of it with the jointer. In the case of a two piece neck, cut two pieces to 27" or so long. If you have a great piece of wood that is 26" go for it. However, it will have to have a small peghead, and it is essential that it have no major cracks or flaws at either end. Before ripping check to make sure that your workpiece has a straight edge on it. If it does not you will have to give it a straight edge with the jointer.

Below: Testing a workpiece against the jointer bed for trueness.

Below: The two halves of a two piece neck with a very thin piece of black veneer which will be glued in between them to accent the glue joint.

2. Rip each piece to 3.25" wide or a little less with the table saw, the extra .25" is to allow for "trueing" with the jointer. If the plan is to make a very deep rim, then cut the pieces wider to allow for it.

3. Look at your lumber again, Are there twists or warps you did not see before? Think on it some more. Lay the pattern on the workpieces again. Test the trueness of your workpieces against the jointer bed or some other very straight thing. Look at the trueness of the width as well as the trueness of the thickness. Most all lumber needs to be trued, so do that with the

jointer now. **Take care to set the cut to be very light at first**. True at least three sides, the side that will be the back of the workpiece need not be trued if you plan to make a single neck. Scribbling on the surface to be trued with a pencil is a handy technique that will allow you to see where the jointer is hitting and where it is not. Check your progress between each pass on the jointer. When you are done all the scribble should be gone. **A live demonstration on jointer safety from a wood working professional is highly recommended.**

4. If you made a one piece workpiece you can skip ahead to the side profile neck layout. Otherwise put the two pieces together in the way they will be glued together and have a look, how is it? Do they match up pretty good? Do the gluing faces fit together solidly? This is important to the long term life of the neck so take your time and look it over really good. Next, look at the surfaces that will become the front profile, the sides intended to be the gluing surface for the fingerboard. The goal here is to create a flat plane from these two pieces. They should be as level with each other as possible, although they will likely have to be trued on the jointer after gluing them together. If you plan to accent the glue joint with a veneer, get it ready. Get the c-clamps ready by opening them up to accommodate the thickness of the workpiece. Plan to stagger the placement of the clamps so that pressure will be applied evenly.

5. Spread the glue onto the mating surface of one of the workpieces. If you are accenting the glue joint, spread glue on the mating surfaces of both workpieces. This can be a slippery operation so having a friend on hand can be helpful. Put the workpieces together. Get the surfaces of the workpieces that the fingerboard will be glued to as even as possible. I like to begin by putting a clamp on one end, tightening a little bit, aligning and tightening some more. Work your way down the workpiece adjusting as necessary. Make sure that there is glue squeezing out all around, and that the fingerboard face is as level as possible, check the ends to make sure they are lined up pretty good. Snug up the clamps and let it sit for a while.

6. After the glue has had a chance to set remove the clamps and take a look. Look up and down the length of the workpiece. Do you see any irregularities? Examine the glue joint. If there is a small gap it may be possible to close it with a clamp and some more glue. Take a look down the fingerboard face of the workpiece. Is it fairly even and level? True the fingerboard face on the jointer to be absolutely sure that the fingerboard will have a flat and even gluing surface. True the sides. It is okay for the back side of the neck to be completely uneven for now. If the ends are uneven, trim them with a saw.

The neck billet after gluing and clamping.

Side Profile Neck Layout

To lay out the side profile of the neck, a straight edge, protractor, and square come in handy. If you don't have a pattern and think you may make more than one banjo, now might be a good time to make a pattern. I have just one pattern for both 11" and 12" necks. I just add a 1/2" to the length of the neck for an 11" rim, the neck in that case being slightly longer. Take a peek in the Patterns and Jigs section for a photo of the neck patterns. In its most basic representation the side profile neck layout consists of three rectangles; one for the peghead, one for the neck, and one for the heel, keep this in mind as you figure out the layout for the first time.

1. Have your figures handy from your scale length considerations. For a 12" rim I usually allow 19" for the length of the fingerboard, in the case of an 11" rim I use 19.5" for the fingerboard length. It is just fine to leave the workpiece a bit long at this point. In fact the workpiece should be a little long on the end that will meet the rim. Measure from the end of the workpiece or pattern material that will be the heel of the neck. Use the straight edge along the side of the workpiece that has been trued by the jointer as the line that represents the fingerboard. Mark it at the correct length. In the case you are marking directly on the workpiece, leave a little extra length.

2. At the heel end of the neck, use the protractor to mark a line at 87 degrees perpendicular to the surface that will be the fingerboard. This line can be as long as the workpiece is wide for the present, it represents the angle that the heel of the neck will be cut at.

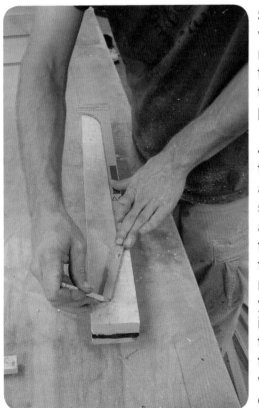

3. It is fine for the heel to be the full width of the workpiece for now. Measure up from the line you just marked about 3" and then mark a line parallel to the fingerboard surface. There are a variety of ways that the heel of a banjo neck can taper into the handle portion of the neck, I like to use a gentle curve.

4. Now let's layout the peghead. I like my pegheads to tilt back from the plane of the fingerboard at about 7 degrees. Use the protractor and the surface that represents the fingerboard to find the angle. Between six and seven inches long is fine for the peghead. I usually cut out my peghead to a thickness that will accommodate the tuning machines. If you have one of the machine tuners you intend to use, measure it carefully, or try fitting it to a piece of scrap wood to get an idea of the total thickness the peghead will need to be. It is important to consider the thickness of the peghead overlay when planning the thickness of the peghead. If you do not intend to use an overlay, the thickness of the

peghead can be the same as your measurement from the tuner. If you do intend to use an overlay the peghead will have to be thinner than your measurement or test piece. To arrive at the correct thickness simply subtract the thickness of the peghead overlay from the measurement or thickness of the test piece. I would recommend that the peghead *never* be any thinner than 3/8", after sanding and leveling, in the case that you intend to use a peghead overlay and the overlay is 1/8" thick. In the case that you do not intend to use an overlay, no thinner than a 1/2" after sanding and leveling. Draw a rectangle of the appropriate dimensions for your plan. Using the line that meets the line for the fingerboard as the long side that will be the face of the peghead mark the back side of the peghead by making a line parallel to the first.

5. Mark the neck to be 1" thick where the peghead meets the backside of the neck. The neck gets thicker as it nears the heel. At the place where the neck meets the heel, the neck should be 1.5" thick. Draw a straight line to mark the backside of the neck.

6. When you are satisfied with your layout, saw it out with the band saw. Don't cross the line but saw right up to it. It is okay if the peghead is a little thick at this point as it will still have to be sanded flat. A little of the thickness may be removed at that time.

7. At this point the side profile has been cut out. I now call this workpiece a neck blank. Save the extra pieces that were sawn out from the backside of the neck as they may be handy for making "ears" and the dowel stick later on. It is often a good idea to let the neck "rest" a while at this point. After removing so much wood from the back of the neck the new shape can bend in response to its own internal pressures in ways that it bound itself from bending before. That is, a twist in the wood which has gone unseen up to this point may now become active because the wood that has been removed from the backside of the neck no longer restricts it. Its moisture content may also change. Lay aside the workpiece for a few days or weeks. In the summertime I often cure mine in a hot car for a few days at this point to cook out any moisture. This is double important when working with figured woods! As the variety in the grain makes for beautiful patterns, it may also create unseen tension which can do unexpected things. Give it the time it takes to cure properly. Then, after some time for curing, eyeball it and check it against the jointer bed to be sure that it is still true. If you find that the neck blank has warped or twisted in any way, use the jointer to very carefully return the fingerboard surface to a flat even plane. It is also important to consider the angle where the peghead surface meets the fingerboard surface. The point at which the peghead breaks from the fingerboard should be consistent. Marking a line square to the long side of the fingerboard gluing surface to represent the breakpoint across the width of the fingerboard surface can act as a good guide.

Reinforcing the Neck

It's a good idea to reinforce your banjo necks for long term stability and playability. There are different ways to reinforce a neck. I use 1/8" thick by 1/2" wide hot rolled steel bar stock to reinforce my necks. It can be found at most hardware stores. Some builders prefer to use truss rods. Truss rods may offer some advantage as they can be adjusted, thereby changing the relief (intentional bow) of the neck. However, truss rods may also leave some air space inside the neck which may have some effect on the over all tone and responsiveness of the banjo. The steel bar stock leaves no empty space inside the neck and may produce a more resonant instrument. Having never made a banjo with a truss rod I won't go into detail on that. Today there is also the option of using a graphite bar instead of steel. Graphite is very light, rigid, and strong.

The neck will have to have a channel cut into it to accommodate the steel or graphite bar. I use the table saw to cut the channel, it usually takes two passes, just a little apart from each other, and set low enough that the bar will sit flush with the jointed surface of the neck. This leaves only 1/4" to 1/2" of wood between the reinforcement bar and the back of the neck, some of which will be carved away, so be very careful not to saw too deep. This job may also be accomplished with a router. If you like you might do a test run on a piece of scrap. I try to center my channel as much as possible. In the photo at the bottom of the page, it can be seen that the ends of the steel bar are cut out for tabs that hold it in place while gluing. This is a process that Mac picked up from Kyle Creed some years ago. The bar is set into the neck using epoxy.

A 3 piece neck blank with a channel cut for reinforcement.

1. Cutting the steel. I usually cut my steel about an inch or so shorter than the length of the fingerboard. A hack saw does the job okay, but it will go a lot easier with a jig saw that has a metal cutting blade.

2. Mac usually cuts a ledge in the ends of the bar so that wooden tabs may be fashioned to cinch the steel into place when gluing. The tabs are wider than the steel at this point, leaving them to sit above the surface of the fingerboard plane when inserted in the channel. I have tried the job without the tabs, using small pieces of waste steel to hold the bar in place. Both procedures work well; however, I still used wood to fill in the ends of the channel. The channel in the neck runs the length of it. If you are using a plunge router you may be able to cut a channel that does not need tabs to fill in the ends.

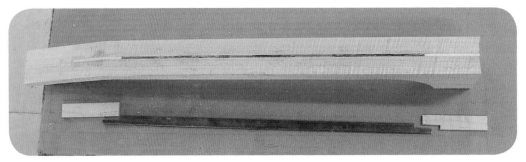

3. Test the fit of the steel. It should be snug but not tight. If it is too tight then go back to the table saw and zip off a tiny bit more wood from inside the channel. Be sure that the top edge of the bar does not sit above the level of the fingerboard gluing surface. It should not stick up at all, but it should not sit down in the channel too much either.

4. Mix the epoxy and put some in the channel. It need not be full as the bar will take up most of the space in there, but be sure to use enough to get plenty of "squeeze out".

5. Put in the bar and push it into place with the tabs or with your fingers. Clamp the tabs and use scrap steel as a caul to get clamping pressure on the bar in the middle of the neck. Avoid marring the fingerboard gluing surface with the clamps.

6. Wipe away the extra epoxy quick as you can. There may be a little left on there which will have to be scraped off or chiseled off later. That's okay.

7. Let the epoxy set for however long it should. I like the 5 minute kind, then remove the clamps. Carefully knock off the caul steel if it is stuck on there. Remove the extra epoxy while it is soft with a scraper or a chisel.

8. Give the epoxy time to fully set, then trim off the protruding wooden tabs with a chisel.

Ears

In the case that the fingerboard surface of my workpiece was less than 3" wide, I'll probably want to put some ears on the peghead to make it a little wider. The ears are small pieces of wood that are the length of the peghead, the thickness of the peghead, and as wide you would like to make them. There is no need to add a lot of width to the peghead. Just add enough to make room for the peghead design you intend to use. I use the scrap I saved from the portion of the neck workpiece that I cut away when cutting out the side profile of the neck. It may be necessary to true one of the surfaces of this workpiece on the jointer so there will be a truly flat side to glue to the sides of the peghead. Cut the ears to the thickness of the peghead and glue them on the sides. It is likely that both the front and back sides of the peghead will have to be leveled after this step, so don't worry if your ears are a tiny bit thicker, or thinner than the peghead or slightly misaligned. Cutting them as close as you can to the correct thickness will save work later. With most figured woods, it is difficult to see whether ears are used or not, they usually don't stand out. I like to use them, as it is a practice which saves wood in the long run. This practice also allows me to begin with thinner stock, some of which is very beautiful. When the ears have been glued on, the peghead looks really big and bulky. It is usually necessary to level the peghead at this time. I usually do it with a sander, or a sanding plate but have also done it with a rasp and file. If you use a power sander for this operation, go slow and be very careful to keep the thickness consistent.

The ears before and after gluing.

The neck blank with peghead overlay and fingerboard attached.

Peghead Overlay

The next job is the peghead overlay. The overlay is a thin piece of wood matching the fingerboard, rim cap, and heel cap. A peghead overlay is not an essential element of the banjo. They are usually used as an accent feature. If you do not intend to accent the rim cap, or the heel cap, there is no need to accent the peghead either. The peghead overlay may be left off entirely so long as the peghead is thick enough and you are satisfied with the look. I like to add accent features, so I'll give some detail about the overlay. One end of the peghead overlay will meet the fingerboard. There are two ways for the overlay to meet the fingerboard.

1.
One way is for the end of the overlay to continue right up to the place where the peghead breaks from the fingerboard plane, and then level it off to match the plane of the fingerboard. With this option the fingerboard will overlap or nearly overlap the end of the overlay. The nut will sit on top of the overlay. If this is your choice, it must be done before the fingerboard is glued on.

2.
The other way is to bevel the edge of the overlay that will meet the fingerboard to run perpendicular to the plane of the fingerboard. If you choose this option, the overlay will be glued on right up to the place where the peghead breaks from the fingerboard plane. When the fingerboard is glued on, a small gap will be left between the overlay and the fingerboard. Later on this will hold the nut. This solution can be seen in the photo at left.

The peghead overlay should be cut a little bigger than the pattern for the shape of the peghead and glued onto the peghead after the peghead has been leveled. Take care to center the overlay on the peghead. Use cauls to keep from marring the wood and spread the clamping pressure evenly, it's a wide flat area so take care to get a positive bond all the way across. Mac drills 1/16" holes in the scrap area and tacks on the overlay with small brads to keep it from shifting during gluing. The brads can be removed after positive clamping pressure is achieved.

Fingerboard

I prefer that my fingerboard, peghead overlay, heel cap, and rim cap match. It is a nice point of style, although there have been times when I used wood that matched the neck for everything but the fingerboard. The traditional choices for fingerboards are ebony or rosewood. I like ebony best but rosewood is okay too. Why not just use the same wood that the rest of the banjo is made from? Well, it's typically not hard enough. The fingerboard takes a lot of wear from the fingers. That being the case, it is wise to have a fingerboard that is as hard as possible. This makes for a long life in an instrument.

To fret, or fret not?

I like to play both the fretted and fretless banjo. They are however, very different instruments. The fretless fingerboard is easier to make but harder to play. The fretted fingerboard demands some very exact measurement and cutting but is usually considered to be a little friendlier to the beginning player. I have purchased pre-slotted fingerboards from luthier supply houses in the past. I have also cut my own fret slots. I like to lay out the slots using an IBEX fret rule. Mac lays out his slots using a fingerboard from a bashed up guitar. I like to buy the pre-slotted fingerboards when I can. They are good, cut out by a CNC router and play precisely. I feel the money I pay for them is worth it as it is easy to make a small mistake when slotting, small enough that it may not be noticeable to the eye but will be noticeable to the ear when the instrument is strung up and played for the first time. However, I'll go over fret slotting here because it is good to do it at least once. It is much easier to cut the fret slots before gluing the fingerboard to the neck.

Slotting

I use the Ibex fret rule for marking out the fret spacing. It is possible to use the fingerboard of a currently playing instrument to develop the fret spacing if you can figure out a good way to hold it and can mark VERY precisely. The fingerboard needs to have a straight edge so that a square may be used to layout the lines across the fingerboard. Check the edge of your fingerboard material, true it up with the jointer if necessary. I like to use a clamping arrangement on a table with a square to help me keep the slots in the right place. I also use a fret saw that has a stop to prevent me from sawing the slots too deep. It is also of great importance that the fret slots be of the correct width to hold the tang of the fret wire. If it happens that a fret turns out to be a little off after the banjo is strung up for the first time, the slot can be filled with a dust/epoxy mixture and recut. Save some of the dust that results from cutting slots. If the dust is not used here it can be used at the time of inlay work. It would be a shame to lose a whole fingerboard over one small mis-cut slot. Mac sometimes uses a slotting jig to cut his slots, the design for which I believe came from a book we had around for a while by Robert Benadetto, the great arch-top guitar builder. It uses the waste from an old fingerboard and a pin to increment the spacing of the frets.

Gluing on the fingerboard is much like gluing on the peghead overlay, only bigger. Before gluing make sure everything under there is right. Be sure that the mating surfaces are clean, true, and as free from chips as possible. Take care to align the fingerboard properly with the peghead overlay. Again use the clamps and cauls. Again, brads may be used to prevent slipping while clamping.

Fretless

In the case that you choose to go fretless there is no need to bother with thinking about fretting, it is fine to leave the fretboard as it is. However, some fretless banjos feature a brass plate which covers the first to fifth or seventh fret area on the fingerboard. It is a nice touch and I feel it makes playing a little easier in the case of steel strings. For nylon strings I prefer to have only the wood of the fingerboard. It is easy to add a brass plate to the fingerboard. Find some thin brass plate, perhaps at a hobby shop or a store that carries supplies for architectural models. Cut out the brass to roughly the shape that you desire. Make sure the end that will meet the nut is straight. It is okay for the brass to be a little wider than the fingerboard. If you want to add any decorative shape to the end of the plate nearest the bridge you should do it before fixing it to the fretboard. I rough up the mating sides of the fingerboard and the plate with some 150 grit sandpaper. Then I attach the plate using epoxy and cauls. After the epoxy is dry you can file down the plate to the exact dimensions of the fingerboard.

Neck Heel Dowel Stick Hole

Take some time to think over your measurements really good before you drill this hole. It may be helpful to look back at the location of the Dowel Stick Holes section in Early Considerations, page 5. The dowel stick hole can be drilled either before or after the neck has had its radius cut. It is typically drilled using a jig with the Shop Smith or the drill press, and a 3/4" forstner bit. The jig holds the neck so that the dowel stick hole comes in at the same angle that the neck meets the rim, about 3 degrees. It

Top: A fretless banjo neck with a scoop.

At Left : The neck heel dowel stick hole.

is important to keep it straight, as a crooked hole makes for a crooked dowel stick. **It is also important that this hole be drilled at the correct angle.** At this stage I like to cut the heel of the neck to the correct angle, but leave it flat on the edge that will meet the rim. That way I can use a square to see that the forstner bit is drilling at the correct angle. When the neck is in the jig the forstner bit should come in at 90 degrees to the mating side of the heel. Try to drill the hole in one go, as multiple attempts could misshape the hole, resulting in a loose fitting stick. Make the hole at least 1.5" or a little deeper, but be careful not to drill completely through the other side of the neck heel.

Adding a Radius and Angle to the Heel
Important stuff!

In order to make stringed instruments more playable nearly all of them have the neck attached at an angle. Fiddles, cellos, guitars, and yes, even banjos have a small angle built into the neck/body joint. This small angle allows for essential adjustment to take place. It also increases the angle of the strings across the bridge. The sharper the angle of the string across the bridge the more downward pressure is communicated to the head. Too sharp an angle is not so good as it can result in an instrument sounding too "lively". Too flat an angle is not so good either as it may render the instrument dull. Fiddles often sport a neck angle of seven degrees, many flat top guitars are one degree. My favorite banjos have a neck angle of 3 degrees. 3 degrees allows for a bridge height that I find to be ideal for clawhammer playing, not too high or too low, about 5/8" tall.

Cutting this angle is complicated in the case of the banjo by the fact that the neck will be attached to a round hoop. It is structurally and acoustically important that this joint have a good fit. So not only should it be angled but it also must have a radius that is cut at the proper angle to fit the hoop and deliver the desired playability.

The **Neck heel radius jig** is used to assist in cutting the heel of the neck so that it will mate cleanly with the rim. It helps us cut an angle and a radius at the same time. It consists of a plate that screws or clamps onto the saw table of a band saw. The plate of

the jig has two halves, one half has a convex arc and the other has a concave arc. The arc should have a diameter a tiny bit less than the diameter of the rim you intend to use. On the side of the plate that has the concave arc there should be a wedge that will hold the neck at 3 degrees from the plane of the plate. This jig can be made from wood or it could be made from metal.

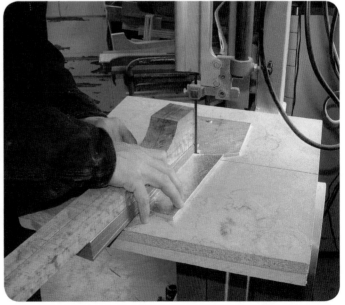

After cutting the radius with the band saw a sanding wheel jig may be used to get all the saw marks out of the heel of the neck. This also allows us to adjust our radius and angle a little bit. I have also done the job by hand with a piece of sand paper attached to the waste cut off the heel of the neck. It is best to wait for this part of the job until the rim has been turned on the lathe. Waiting allows the actual pieces to be fit together at near finished dimensions and make totally sure that the fit is good. If you choose to use a sanding wheel, it is usually best to use one that is of a smaller diameter than that of the rim.

It is very important that these jigs be constructed well and used properly. Use some scrap to test your work. If the neck is mounted on the jig crooked the neck will be crooked when it is mounted on the banjo. This is a mistake I have made and although it may still result in a playable banjo, people will look at you funny. It is a good idea to have a good sharp blade on the bandsaw for this job. The sharper the blade the less sanding will need to be done. If you're doing the sanding by hand, take good care not to modify the radius or the angle.

Neck Heel Tension Hoop Rabbet

This area allows the tension hoop to sit down over the rim. It makes a space for the tension hoop at the place where the neck meets the rim and can be seen clearly on page 5. It is cut with the router using a jig that can be developed using the tension hoop itself.

Seen below: The tension hoop rabbet jig. The underside is seen at left and the end that the router will bear against is seen at right.

The tension hoop rabbet should be as near to the thickness of the tension hoop as possible. It should be deep enough to allow the tension hoop to be tightened fully, which is usually a little greater than 1/2". The jig should be built with a wedge so that the tension hoop rabbet will reflect the angle of the neck.

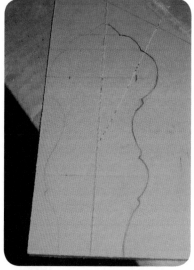

Above: A peghead design laid out on a piece of plexi-glass which will be made into a template.

Laying out the Peghead

The peghead presents an opportunity to show off some creative flair. There are many attractive peghead designs out there and it is easy to come up with one's own. All this aside, the peghead has a job to do. It holds the tuning machines and so must have room to accommodate them without crowding. So, before I get my heart set on a design, I first consider how much room my tuners are apt to take. There are several styles of tuners available commercially with varying sizes of shaft diameter and height. I like to get my tuners before I settle on a peghead design, just to check it all out. I have found that allowing the diameter of a 25 cent piece leaves plenty of room for most commercial tuners. When I'm designing a new peghead I use the quarter as a layout tool to find a workable spacing for my tuners. After the shape is figured out it can be transferred to the peghead. Be sure to mark the centers of the peghead holes at this time as well. Later these marks will tell us where to drill the hole that the tuners will sit in.

At Right: The front profile of the neck roughed out.

Laying out the front profile of the neck

The front profile of the neck represents the available space for playing. I believe Mac has developed his own patterns from vintage banjo fingerboards. It is a good idea to use a pattern or another banjo as a template for this part of the design as the front profile of the banjo is an irregular shape. There are two ways to think of the front profile of the banjo neck. It could be thought of as a four string neck with a fifth string bump out beginning part of the way down, or it could be thought of as being a five string neck all the way up to the nut with the fifth string area cut out above the fifth fret. Why does it matter? Because the placement of a center line changes with each perception. It is a good idea to develop a center line for laying out and thinking of shapes, even in the case of asymmetric shapes. It helps with lining things up. So where is the center line on a 5 string banjo fingerboard? Well, the Mac solution is to measure half the width of the fingerboard at the nut end of the neck and half the width of the fingerboard at the rim end of the neck and draw a straight line connecting the two. This line should basically follow the center line of a laminated neck blank.

The neck blank with peghead overlay and fingerboard attached. The cradle assists in holding the neck while band sawing.

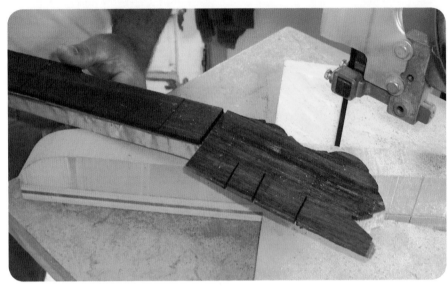

The front profile of the neck begins to take shape. The cradle helps to cut the sides of the peghead so that the contour lines are ninety degrees to the plane of the fingerboard.

After both the peghead and front profile of the neck are laid out it is time to visit the band saw. Mac uses a "cradle" to hold the neck with the fingerboard facing up and sitting level. This helps cut the peghead so that the contour lines of it's sides are ninety degrees perpendicular to the plane of the fingerboard rather than the plane of the peghead, a small detail reminiscent of many golden era banjos. The cradle also makes the job a lot easier and safer.

After band sawing, the fingerboard pattern or template is fixed to the fingerboard with double sided tape or small screws. The neck is put in the vice and the template is routed around to clean up all the rough stuff left over by the bandsaw. In many cases I have simply worked it down by hand with the rasp at this point, working to a line that marks out the shape of the neck.

Trimming Peghead Thickness
This is a good time to check to make sure that the peghead is not too thick to

accommodate the tuners. You can measure or just hold the tuner up to the thick side of the peghead. If it looks as though they will not be tall enough for the bushing bolt and washer to get on the shaft by a few turns the peghead will likely have to be thinned down. There are several ways to accomplish this task at this point. The job can be done by hand with a rasp. It can also be done using a fence on the bandsaw. A power sander may also be used. Take care not to get the peghead too thin.

Drilling the Peghead Holes

The peghead holes are where the tuners will mount to the peghead. They should be of the proper diameter to hold the tuner shafts. Measure carefully and select a dill bit of the correct size. A brad point drill bit can be very helpful in getting the location accurate. Do a test hole on some scrap wood. It is also a good idea to have some kind of backing behind the workpiece to minimize tear-out which is often a problem at this step. The tuner holes will be drilled at 90 degrees to the plane of the peghead. The tuner shaft should be snug but not tight. If you have to struggle to get it in, the hole is too small. If the tuner is a little loose in the hole that is okay, but not very loose as a snug fit is best. Experiment with different size bits until you find one that is just right.

Holding the neck in place while drilling the tuner holes can be tough, but is essential. It is fine to drill the tuner holes from either side of the peghead, but be sure to use some kind of backing material to minimize tear out. Mac has a jig he built just for this purpose. The job can be done without a jig as well. A steady handed friend can be a big help.

Sanding the Contours of the Peghead

Another cradle type jig is used in this operation, or possibly the same jig that was used to cut out the peghead profile. As with the bandsaw it allows for steady holding and keeps the angles consistent. Mac uses a small sanding drum chucked into the drill press to sand the curved areas.

Shaping the Neck

This is a great part of making the banjo. I like to do it all by hand. Here we remove all the rough square edges left by the saws and round the neck to its final shape. Don't forget there is a steel bar in there! Going too deep is a sure way to turn your banjo neck into firewood! Give it the time it takes and go slow. I use a drawknife and chisels at the beginning; the drawknife for the length of the neck and the chisels for the heel and fifth peg area. It is wise to have your tools very sharp here. With figured woods like curly or birds-eye maple it is easy to tear out a big chunk without meaning to. Try to orient the neck and your own position so that you are not pulling into the grain, but pulling with the grain of the wood. I use the big tools to hog off the big rough corners. I really like this part of the job so I may tend to savor it, I switch to the rasp and file pretty early. The place where the fifth string bumps out from the rest of the neck gives an opportunity for carving some personal embellishment. It is good place for signature details.

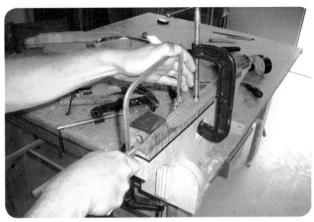

Roughing out the neck heel with the coping saw

Working off the rough corners with the drawknife

Final shaping with the rasp and file

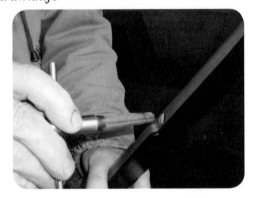

Reaming out the fifth peg hole

Fifth Peg Hole

The fifth peg hole holds the fifth string tuning machine, sometimes called the fifth peg. This is a hole in the side of the neck just above the fifth string bump out. Take a look at your fifth string machine tuner and you will likely find that it features a tapered and knurled shaft which will be pressed into the hole that will be drilled into the side of the neck. Look at the small end of the knurled shaft, find a drill bit that matches that diameter. The neck will have to be set on its edge on the drill press table. I usually just hold it in place with the hand that is not operating the press lever, but work up a clamping arrangement if you wish. Go easy and don't use too much pressure. Remember the bar of hot rolled steel we put in there? It's okay to bump up against it but don't drill through it. Be careful of the angle of the neck if you are holding it by hand as it may have a tendency to roll as pressure is applied by the bit which could end with the drill bit coming out of the surface of the fingerboard. Pay close attention to the feel of the press lever.

After drilling, the hole has to be tapered to accept the tapered shaft of the peg. Mac uses a 5 degree tapered reamer that has had the narrowest portion removed to do the job. Turn it gently and check your progress often. If you taper carefully you will not have to epoxy the fifth peg in place, it will hold itself. However, don't let that idea be too important, it is possible to crack a neck by forcing the peg into a hole that is too small for it.

Pip Hole

The pip is a miniature nut that serves the fifth string. The pip is usually cylinder shaped and made from the same material as the nut. I make mine to be about 1/8" diameter at the biggest. The edge nearest the bridge should come out either even with or just behind the fifth fret. Drill the hole in the face of the fingerboard and be careful not to go too deep. It's possible to drill through to the backside of the neck!

Adding the Scoop

My fretted banjos typically have only seventeen frets. Above the seventeenth fret I like to "scoop" the neck. The scoop allows for easier playing on the neck, yielding a mellower tone that I really enjoy. I do the job with the belt sander or with a rasp and file. I like to take that area of the fingerboard down to a little less than half of it's original thickness.

Inlay

Inlay work deserves a whole book of its own, but I'll go over it a bit. Mac often cuts his own inlay by hand. Unique one of a kind design work can be achieved in this way. If you choose to cut your own inlay use a dust mask. Dust from mother of pearl and abalone are toxic! It is a slow process to cut one's own inlay, but fun! Pre-cut inlay materials are available from various sources as well. The most common materials for inlay work are mother of pearl and abalone. Many other materials such as, bone, wood, or metal may be inlaid as well.

Installing pre-cut inlay is pretty easy. In the case of little round circles it is as easy as drilling a shallow hole that the dots can sit in. In the case of diamonds or some other shape the router will likely be necessary. However, if you are very good with a chisel you may have no need of a router.

First work out your designs on paper. It is a good idea to make photo copies of your designs before you cut them out, for future reference. Cut them out and have a look at them on the banjo. Look good? I use spray adhesive to fix the paper designs to the mother of pearl or abalone blanks. A jeweler's saw is the tool of choice for cutting mother of pearl and abalone. Cut the shapes out as near as possible. Don't be discouraged if some break, just try again. Use a needle file to knock off any rough places left by the saw.

Routing

I use a dremel tool with a very small bit and a precision router base to make the holes for the inlay pieces. Lay out the cut and filed inlays on the fingerboard. Use something sticky to hold them in place. Carefully trace around them with a scribing tool. Then remove the inlay pieces and dust the inlay surface with white chalk or shop dust to make the outlines stand out.

Check the depth of cut on the dremel against the thickness of the inlay pieces. Do a test piece first. It is okay for the pearl to sit a little proud of the piece being inlaid, but only a little. If you're satisfied that the depth is right, go for it. Be very careful and run the dremel at full speed. If some of the holes come out a little big that is okay, they can be filled. After all the holes are cut, use some epoxy or glue to anchor the inlay in place.

Filling

Collect some dust from whatever kind of wood you are inlaying into. The finer the dust the better. Mix the dust with some clear epoxy, not too thick, but be sure to get plenty of color in it. Use this mixture to fill in any gaps between the edges of the holes and the pearl that was just glued into the work piece.

Leveling

After all the filler is in and set, level the face of the work piece. I use a long, trued by the jointer, piece of hardwood scrap with some 220 sand paper glued on it for the job of leveling. Once the leveling is done you may notice some voids left by air bubbles. Fill those in with more epoxy/dust and level again. After all of the air bubbles are filled sand level with 220 and then progress to finer and finer grades of sandpaper. Continue up to 600 grit and then follow with fine steel wool.

Joining the Dowel to the Neck

It is a good idea to join the dowel stick to the neck before fretting. After the frets are on the surface of the fingerboard will no longer be flat, making it more difficult to clamp it to a jig for possible modifications. Skip ahead to the dowel section for full details.

Side Dot Markers

It is nice to mark the frets on the side of the neck as well as on its face. Very small mother of pearl dots may be used or plastic may be used. For either one drill a small hole the size of the dot and then fill if necessary.

Fret Work

I could go on and on about fret work, it too deserves its own book. I'll just touch on the basics here. Fret wire comes either in a coil or in long straight pieces. The coil is okay for softer wire but when it comes to stiffer wire I prefer it to come in a straight piece. I like medium banjo/mandolin wire. It is narrow and tall enough to allow for leveling and crowning, and likely a re-crowning in the distant future.

To cut the wire to the correct length for each slot just lay the wire next to the slot, plan on cutting it a little long. Hold your place on the fret wire with your thumb and use a pair of side cutters to make the cut. I like to hold both the piece being cut off and the parent piece in one hand while I make the cut. Otherwise the fret is likely to go flying off to who knows where, possibly in someone's eye.

I cut all the frets and lay them out in order, and then tap them all in as a separate operation. Be sure to check that all of the fret slots are deep enough before you begin. I use a fretting hammer with a brass head on one side and a plastic head on the other. The brass being soft it mars and dents the frets less than some harder material, the plastic side is even softer. A little practice is all it takes to get good at fretting. Some luthiers prefer to press the frets in, an idea that I like the sound of. Some also use a big bag of buck shot to hold the neck in place on the work bench in such a way as not to risk cracking it. I just sit on a stool or in a chair and lay the neck across my legs and use them as a shock absorber.

After all the frets are in place there will be little sharp ends sticking out along the fretboard which have to be filed off. Use a long flat file and round over the ends of the frets so they are not at all square or sharp. You will likely be able to feel little sharp corners on them yet. That's okay for now, they will get their turn with a smaller file after leveling and crowning.

I use much the same technique and even the same tool for leveling the frets as for leveling the fingerboard after inlay: a long hardwood scrap, which has been trued at the jointer, with 220 sandpaper stuck on it. Be sure all the frets are seated properly before you begin. You can see where it has been after every stroke, the highest fret surfaces reveal flat spots. Go easy and slow. After all the crowns look a little less shiny you will know that you have touched them. To see if they are all level lay a straight edge across the frets, if it rocks you know that there is a high fret. If you find a high fret take a good look at it to make sure that it is fully seated in its slot. If it is fully seated use your leveling block to get all the frets level and check again.

Crowning
There are a wide variety of tools available for crowning. It can be useful to tape off the fretboard or use a guard of some kind when crowning as it is easy to gouge the fretboard. Work off the squareness on the crowns left by the leveling. Then run your fingers up and down the edges of the neck and feel for sharp edges. A needle file comes in handy here. I have one which I modified for the job. It has a safe edge with no file on it which allows me to file the fret right up to the fingerboard without filing into the fingerboard. Care still must be exercised when using this tool as it is easy to mar the wood surrounding the fret. After all that, buff the neck with some fine steel wool. This will shine the frets, clean up the finger board, and brighten the inlay.

30 The Neck

The Rim

Mac builds his rims by bending long strips of wood and laminating them together using a form. Typically each rim has four strips laminated together. The two interior laminations that do not show are usually straight grained maple, which bends well and is nice and strong. Hickory is also a good choice for the interior laminations of the rim. It's okay to use different wood for the interior laminations than what is used for the exterior. This allows for better use of the figured woods where they may be seen. The exterior laminations that show usually match the neck. After all the strips are laminated, it is likely that the depth of the new rim will have to be trimmed up on the table saw. Then, it gets a rim cap that typically matches the fingerboard and peghead.

Ripping Strips

I have done this as a table saw operation and as a band saw operation. The aim is to get strips that are about 45" long by 3" wide by 3/16" to 1/4" thick. 3/4" lumber is fine to start with, you can get about 3 strips of 3/16" thickness out of a piece that thick, as some is lost to the thickness of the saw blade. In the case of the table saw I encourage the use of a feather board to help hold the piece against the fence. I also encourage the use a push stick.

Ripping strips on the table saw, note the feather board.

Thickness Sanding

After sawing, the strips are still pretty rough. They need to be a bit smoother for the gluing that will soon take place. They also need to have fairly regular dimensions. A thickness sander is ideal for this operation, however, they may be rare to come by. It is possible to make a holding jig for a hand held sander that will also accomplish the job tolerably well. This job can be done with a block plane as well. They need not be super smooth. As a matter of fact a little rough might be good. I like to sand to at least 150 grit.

Bending

Bending wood seems a little mysterious at first, but gets easier to believe after having done it for oneself. There are several ways to bend wood: boiling, steaming, and ammonia treatment. Boiling is the way that I have done it with the most success. After boiling

Soaking strips in the bathtub

Boiling strips on the stove

The heated aluminum hoop with a strip clamped to it. This drives the moisture deep into the wood

Rolling the boiled and steamed strip onto a wooden spool for drying

Mac takes account of the fruits from a full day of strip bending

they are bent against a thick aluminum hoop that is heated on the stove. This drives the moisture into the wood and makes a nice gentle curve. At times I have skipped the aluminum ring step, using only plywood spools for bending. However, the more highly figured a strip is, the hotter it needs to be. I like to have some way of driving the moisture deeper into the wood. After bending on the aluminum ring it is good to roll the strips up onto a plywood spool to allow the bend to "set". Each plywood spool is about 10" in diameter and about four inches tall with a mouth cut into it to accept an end of the strip. They also have holes drilled into them to facilitate clamping the rolled strip. An old piece of guttering works well for a boiling pan as it is long and narrow. It can be heated on a Coleman stove or set across the burners of a kitchen stove.

Strip bending from the beginning;

1. The sanded strips are soaked in water over night to get them as saturated as possible.

2. Put the strips in the pan and get it boiling hot, the strips float less when they have reached maximum saturation.

3. Have tongs and gloves handy for handling the strips when they are hot enough. Also wear a thick shirt, the operation of rolling the strips onto the spools often needs some help from the belly. If you have one, use the heated metal ring to make the initial bend. Then roll up the strip onto one of the plywood spools. Clamp it in place and leave sit until it is cooled off a little.

4. After cooling remove the strip and tie it up with some twine or string, hang it up to dry for a while.

When bending strips it is common to break some in the process, others will end up with split ends. That's normal and should be planned for. There is a bit of set up involved in bending so why not do several strips while you're at it, at least six or seven.

Forming the Rim

Forming the rim requires the use of the rim clamping form. The inside dimension of the form matches the outside dimension of the rim. The form I use is made in two pieces so that the rim can pop right out. Mac's rim form uses a latch and a hinge, see the Forms, and Jigs section for a photo. Cauls should be used to bear against the inside of the bent strips to keep the clamps from marring them while forming. This is a clamp intensive process so get all the clamps that you can, I like to have at least 7 or 8 on hand.

1. Fit the strip that you plan to use as the outer most lamination into the form, it should be too long and double over itself at the ends. Use the cauls and clamps to get the strip snug against the wall of the form. Start in the middle and work your way around to each end, when you get there take a look at it and see how much needs to be cut off so that it will make one single layer and will meet itself. Remove the strip and cut it to length. Be a

Finding the correct length

Fitting the second lamination

Gluing the first and second laminations together

little generous with this cut and bevel the ends so they will lap over one another. Keep test fitting and modifying until the beveled ends meet each other as cleanly as possible. If it's not super pretty that may be alright as this joint can be covered by the neck heel. Make it as good as possible, do it as many times as it takes. If it doesn't look too good or comes out too short you can get some practice by using the intended outer strip for the inner strip. I suppose it is possible to make patterns to cut each successive laminating strip if they were all the same thickness every time. I find a bit of variety in my own work so I fit each strip individually. It takes time but comes out nice.

2. For the next laminations repeat the above process leaving the previous laminations in place each time. Get the first two layers fitting good and glue them up before cutting the other layers.

3. It is likely that some of the strips attempted to spiral out of the form, that's okay, so long as they didn't spiral out too far. I would consider more than a 1/4" to be too far, depending on the depth dimension I started with. After all the laminations are glued up the rim can be trimmed on the saw. I like my finished rims to be about 2.5" deep. A little shallower is okay but not much. The case of a rim intended to be used with the tubaphone tone ring is the exception, which could have a bit shallower rim because the tone-ring in that case is so tall.

Rim Cap

If you wish to accent the rim cap, it should match the fingerboard. In the case you don't plan to accent it, it could match the neck. The rim cap covers the laminations that would otherwise be visible on the backside of the rim. The cap is usually made from four or five thin pieces of wood butted together. I like to cut the ends of mine so that they slant into each other. In the case of ebony, the butt joint often becomes nearly invisible. A power sander is handy to have around to help with fitting the joints together. It also helps to cut the cap pieces a bit wider than the rim. This allows for a little play when gluing them in place. Wait until all the others are glued in place and set, then adjust the edges of the final piece to make a nice clean joint on both ends. After the glue has set trim them all near flush with the outside and inside of the rim with a flush cut router bit or use the rasp and file. The rim cap may be put on either before or after the lathe work.

Lathe Work

Now it is time to true the rim on the lathe. The rim is mounted to a wooden plate which is attached to a hub that chucks into the lathe. The rim is mounted to the plate with screws. It needs to be mounted evenly so that it will come out as round as possible. There is some danger of cutting through the outermost layer if the rim is mounted unevenly. Go slowly, trim the outside of the rim as well as the inside, let the lathe do the work and watch out for tear out in the case of figured woods. Take off as little as possible to get the rim to the desired size and shape. Before you begin make a mark on your plate to help center the

rim. The mark can also be used to inform you of when you have gone far enough. While you have it spinning on the lathe take some sand paper and smooth it up. In the case you have no lathe, the rim can be trued somewhat using a combination of the blockplane, the file, and the power sander. **For safety and success, a live demonstration by an experienced wood working professional is a must for beginners at lathe work.**

Cutting the Rim Dowel Stick Hole

The location of the *rim* dowel stick hole is interdependent with the location of the *neck* dowel stick hole. A lot of things come into consideration here, like the height of the tone ring, and the depth of the rim. Also, the neck should cover the place where the outermost lamination of the rim meets itself,

Look closely and the lay out for the rim's dowel stick hole may be seen marked in pencil above the ruler.

so try to center the hole on that joint. I like for the end of the scoop to come just even with the top of the head. On the neck, measure the space from the front of the dowel stick hole to the face of the scoop, this measurement tells us how far back from the top of the tone ring the *rim* dowel stick hole will *begin*. Make note of your measurement. Put the tone ring on or subtract its height from your measurement. Find the joint where the outermost lamination of the rim meets itself, measure parallel with the joint beginning from the front face of the rim and make a mark

according to your measurements. Check it twice. Base the rest of the hole measurements on that, mark it clearly. I typically drill a small hole and then cut it out the rest of the way with a coping saw. Then a file can be used to clean up the edges. The fit of the dowel stick should be snug but not tight, a little loose may be okay but I like snug.

Drilling the Shoe Bolt and End pin Holes

The layout of the shoe bolt holes will depend on the type of tension hoop you have chosen to use. For the notched tension hoop you will have to make the shoe bolt holes match the pre-existing hook spacing on the tension hoop. If you have chosen to use a grooved tension hoop you can chose your own spacing. The layout procedure for the grooved hoop follows. The spacing between each shoe depends on how many hooks are called for. 10 on each side of the rim is a good number that will allow for even tightening of the head. Remember that some of the space on the rim will be taken up by the heel of the neck, rendering that area unavailable for hooks and shoes. The end pin bolt which will hold the dowel to the tail of the rim will also need a hole.

1. Use the square to mark a straight line where the middle of the neck will sit on the rim.

This line should be where the two ends of the outer most laminations of the rim meet. This is where the rim's dowel stick hole is. The line should be near the middle of the hole.

2. Find the opposite of this mark by measuring around the rim with a flexible tape measure or a piece of string. When the measurement or length of string from both directions is the same you know that you have found the opposite side. Mark another straight line at this point. This is where the end pin bolt hole will go.

Drilling the shoe bolt holes. Note the use of a backing block to prevent tear out.

3. Now figure where the hook next to the end pin bolt hole should be. 1.5" is plenty in the case of a 12" rim. Perhaps a little less would be fine as well. Mark it on each side of the end pin bolt hole mark. At this point put the neck on and mark the outline of the heel, then remove the neck. I like to have my first hook about 1/2" - 3/4" or so from the front edge of the neck, mark that too. Use the flexible tape to measure from the mark (not the end pin mark but the first hook mark) at the tail of the rim around to the mark up by the neck, note the measurement and divide it by 10. That gives the hook and shoe spacing.

There are other good ways to arrive at hook spacing. Mac has a jig that he uses with the ShopSmith. It spins on a pivot. I have used a regular drill press for the job as well, marking the spacing as noted above. When drilling through the rim it is good to have some kind of backing to prevent tear out on the inside of the rim. To find the right size drill bit just experiment with scrap and one of the shoe bolts.

The end pin bolt hole is not quite the same as the shoe bolt holes. It has to line up with the dowel that it screws into on the inside of the rim. It generally has the same diameter as the shoe bolt holes. Put the neck in and secure it in place with the neck brace. Mark a square where the tail of the dowel stick touches the inside of the rim. Remove the neck and find the center of the square. Measure carefully and transfer the measurement to the outside of the rim. Make a small hole and put the neck back in to be totally sure it is in the right place. Make sure the hole in the rim and the hole in the dowel line up, if they do go ahead and drill the hole out the rest of the way with correct bit.

The Dowel

The dowel stick brings the neck and the rim together. It is possible to use a steel rod or a pair of steel rods for the dowel. Steel rods are not a bad solution. I use a wooden dowel, as many open back banjo makers do. There may be some tonal variation associated with the use of different materials for the dowel. I prefer to use wood.

You may be able to cut this piece out of the leftovers from the neck blank. The dowel stick begins at 1" x 1" square and should be about 2" longer than the outside diameter of the rim to begin with. Then it is cut 3/4" round at one end using a tenon cutter and a holding jig. The round end fits into the neck's dowel stick hole. Take a look down the length of the neck with the dowel stick in place. Does the stick point off in one direction or the other, is it straight with the neck? If the stick is off center, try turning it 1/4 turn. If that doesn't fix it turn it again. Find some way to mark the dowel so that you will know which way it goes when you want to put it back in later.

After the stick is test fit to the neck, its thickness is trimmed down to 3/4" x 1" to allow the neck brace to slip around it. The 3/4" sides will face the front and back of the banjo. The dowel stick facilitates the use of a neck brace, which helps to hold the heel of the neck tight against the rim. The use of a neck brace requires a small hole for the brace pin that is usually located a little less than 1/2" from the inside surface of the rim. See Early Considerations for a detailed photo. It is best to wait for this step until you have the neck brace, then measure and adjust accordingly. The end pin screw secures the dowel at the other end. The hole that the endpin screw goes into will have to be pre-drilled along the length of the dowel stick, it should be as close to the center of the dowel as possible. Take care to make the hole big enough for the end pin screw, otherwise there is a risk of cracking the dowel. The dowel stick may be tapered on all four sides at the end pin end of the dowel. I like to wait to taper until I'm ready to fit it to the neck and rim. That way if it looks a little crooked in there or something, it can be tapered to one side or the other to create visual symmetry. This solution can be discovered on many older banjos.

Joining the Dowel Stick to the Neck

Joining the dowel stick to the neck can be a tricky maneuver and takes place after the rim has been turned on the lathe and the *rim* dowel stick hole has been cut. It is first essential to check the fit of the dowel stick in the neck and the rim. The dowel stick should fit snugly through the *rim* dowel stick hole with the rectangular portion of the dowel bearing against the sides of the hole. The tenon portion of the dowel should stick out of the rim about 1.5" or a little more. It is important that the rectangular portion of the dowel terminate just below the rim's outer surface. It may be necessary to trim away at the outer corners of this rectangular portion of the dowel with a file or a pocket knife. If the tail end of the dowel is

The tenon cutter and holding jig. A freshly cut dowel stick can be seen in the upper portion of the photo.

The tenon cutter used for the dowel's tenon and the forstner bit used for the neck's dowel stick hole.

too long it will have to be trimmed. You can come very close to finding the correct length of the dowel by inserting it in the rim and measuring the rectangular portion of the dowel that protrudes from the *rim* dowel stick hole and subtracting a little less than that amount from the total length. The flat end, or tail of the dowel that bears against the inside of the rim will need to be rounded to match the curvature of the interior of the rim.

When you have the length of the dowel just right, insert it into the rim and use a screw to secure it in place. Take a look to see if the stick looks centered. Then, set the neck on it and see how it all looks. Does the neck fit snugly against the rim? If not, what is holding it out? Does the dowel stick look straight with the neck? Trim and adjust the dowel stick as necessary. If the dowel looks a little crooked in there it may be remedied with a few licks on the jointer. Be sure to remove wood from the side of the dowel that looks heavy. I leave the portion nearest the neck at the full dimension of 1" x 3/4". I often taper the stick below that on all four sides, but just as often I leave the stick rectangular for its full length. Only a little taper is needed to correct any problems with visual symmetry. Be careful not to taper the stick too much.

If you have found that there is some issue with the radius or angle on the heel of the neck consider it very carefully. In this case it can be helpful to apply a thick layer of chalk to the area of the rim where the heel of the neck bears against it. Set the neck back on after the chalk has been applied and the chalk will rub off on the areas of the heel that contact the rim. These are the high spots and will have to be trimmed away with a file or pocket knife. After trimming check and trim and recheck until the chalk rubs off uniformly onto the mating surface of the neck heel radius. It could also be that the radius is off. If you have plenty of neck heel material, the radius may be recut or re-sanded to make the fit better. If this is the case it is wise to check that your jig is right. Experiment with scrap until your are sure the jig will deliver the correct cut.

After everything is squared away, get ready to join the neck and dowel. Epoxy is my choice for glue in this operation. Finding a good way to hold the neck in place while the epoxy sets can be tough. Long bar clamps may be used. A long, stretchy piece of an inner tube might work as well. Mac makes his dowel stick to fit pretty snug in the neck heel dowel stick hole, so snug that it is difficult for the excess epoxy to squeeze out. So, he drills a relief hole in the heel of the neck to let out the excess epoxy. After the stick and neck are joined he puts on the heel cap.

Leave the dowel stick screwed into the rim and figure out the fit and clamping procedure without the epoxy, that is to say, do a dry run. Before you mix the epoxy get some wax paper and cut a piece about as wide as the rim is deep and 5" or 6" long. Cut a round hole in it that will allow the round end of the dowel stick to fit through it. This will keep any excess epoxy that might squeeze out from bonding the neck to the rim.

Go ahead and mix the epoxy. I like the five minute kind. Put some inside the neck heel dowel stick hole and put some on the tenon end of the dowel stick. Fit the neck down onto the stick and wipe away any extra that squeezes out. Fit it on and clamp it down in whatever way you've found that works. Make sure it is not tilted forward or backward, or rotated in any way. Look at the place where the heel of the neck meets the rim, is it evenly snug? Is the backside of the heel sitting snug? Make sure it is all snug and then let it sit while the epoxy hardens. I usually give it 20 minutes and then take it apart, if you wait too long it may be difficult to remove the neck and dowel stick from the rim as they could become trapped by epoxy squeeze-out on the inside of the rim.

Finishing, Assembly, & Set-up

Sanding

This is the time to get all the rough stuff off. All of the file and saw marks must go. Take your work out into the sunshine and have a good long close look at all of its surfaces. Look inside the rim, and every where else that a scuff might try to hide. Get out the elbow grease for this one. I start with 120 grit sandpaper, if I have a very rough area then 80 grit. Some sanding can be done with machines as long as you are very careful and mindful of the wood you are removing. Before I move on to each successive grit of sandpaper I like to take a good look at the work under a strong light. The sun is the best.

Stain

Dye stains tend to leave the grain more visible than do pigment stains. There are some very good dye stains on the market today. Some are both water and alcohol soluble. I use alcohol to dilute my stain because it does not raise the grain. I tend to go pretty light with stain as I like to accent the grain, not hide it. It's okay to get creative with your choice of stain. I've heard stories of some strange things being used as stain as well as some more normal stuff like black tea. If any water base material is used the grain will raise and will have to be knocked back down with steel wool or very fine sandpaper.

Finishes

Oil finishes are easy to apply by hand and require no special equipment. I also like the satin luster that they provide. Linseed oil is a great stand alone finish, but it will take forever to dry. Put on a coat and let it set for a day, then do another the next day, and the next day. After 3 coats let it dry for a week or until the finish is no longer sticky. I like to use one coat of linseed oil as a sealer, and then top coat with tung oil. There is also a great gun stock finish out there that I like very much called True-Oil. It is a stand alone finish that dries quick and yields a lovely finish.

Nitro-cellulose lacquer is also a fine finish. It is a sprayed on finish that is the standard for commercial instrument producers and is the same finish that graces the surfaces of the great instruments from the 40's. Some special equipment is necessary as well as a very well ventilated area. Lacquers leave a lovely warmth that is really tough and ages beautifully.

After applying one coat of whatever finish you have chosen take a good look at your work, if there are any bumps, dings, or high spots work them down with some steel wool

A two footed banjo bridge made from walnut with a rosewood cap

or a scraper. Keep putting on successive coats until you have reached the desired level of shine. After the final coat you may wish to use some very fine sand paper or steel wool to knock a little of the shine off. In the case of an oil finish, you might give it some time to cure before buffing. Oil finishes take a long time to cure, it will look a lot different in a couple of months.

Nut, pip, & Bridge

The nut and fifth string pip can be made from a variety of materials. For nylon strung fretless banjos I like ebony. For steel strings I usually use bone or antler.

The nut should sit proud of the fingerboard a little bit. The notches in the nut should be evenly spaced and cut to the size of the intended string diameter. I usually rough out the nut, or, two or three of them shortly before I plan to string the banjo up. I wait until that first string-up, the final assembly, to cut the slots into the nut. There are tiny files made to the exact string sizes commercially available, they come in very handy. A fine needle file will often suffice for the job of filing out the string slots as well. It is good to make the initial cuts with a razor saw. For the first and fifth strings the slot made by the razor saw may be enough. As you string it up for the first time fit each slot to the string. Widen the slots just enough to let the string slip through without binding. If you think the slot is really close but the string still seems to be binding, try marking in the slot with a pencil, the graphite will act as a lubricant.

The pip is like a miniature nut just for the fifth string. It can match the material for the nut, or I sometimes use ebony instead. Using ebony for the pip on a steel string banjo will quiet down the fifth string a little bit, which can be a good thing. The pip is typically round and sits in a little hole made just for it on the nut side of the fifth fret. I have seen some banjos that use a flat head screw that acts as the pip, simply letting the fifth string ride over the fifth fret. Some players also enjoy the use of "railroad spikes" to act as a capo for the fifth string. They are called railroad spikes because that is what they are, miniature railroad spikes from model trains. They are installed just behind whichever fret is to be capoed at, this can make switching between tunings on the fly a little easier.

The bridge is fun to make yourself. You can make your own by using some of the scraps left over from band sawing the front profile of the neck, it will already have good hard wood on the top edge. Commercially made bridges are good too. There are a lot of variations on the basic theme of a banjo bridge. The bridge can change the sound of a banjo dramatically. Experiment and have fun!

Final Assembly & Set Up

The final assembly is when all the hard work comes together. This is the time when you get to hear your banjo's first notes.

1. Put the tuning machines on the peghead.

2. Assemble all the rim components, including the shoes, tone ring, and head.

2a. Put each shoe on with its bolt, use a flat washer on the inside of the rim. Snug up the bolts.

2b. Put all the hooks onto the shoes with their nuts.

2c. Put on the tone ring if you have one.

2d. Put on the head, and slip the tension hoop down over it.

2e. Move all the hooks in place so that they grab the tension hoop, take a look to make sure they are all straight. Tighten all the nuts finger tight. Then get the wrench on them and tighten each one a half turn. Use your thumbs to press against the head, feel its tension. Flip or tap the head and listen to its sound. The head will need to be tightened a good bit. Work your way around the rim tightening each nut a 1/2 turn at a time. You should use a star type pattern for tightening, like tightening a wheel on a car. Tap the head and listen after every round. After the instrument is tuned to pitch the head may sag under the pressure of the strings. This means that the head is still too loose. Tighten it a little more. The tension of the head affects the tone of the banjo dramatically.

3. Put the neck and rim together. Put on the neck brace, put in the end pin screw. Use some extra care when tightening the end pin screw. If its corresponding hole in the dowel is too shallow or too small it could crack the dowel. Proceed with care. Put on the tailpiece.

4. If the pip is not in its place then go ahead and put it where it goes, I use a little glue to hold mine in place.

5. The nut may also be put in place. I often use a little glue to make it stay put. It is essential that the strings do not buzz, this may happen at first. If the string slot in either the bridge or nut is too loose for the string, that string may buzz. I like to set the action from the nut with the nut in place on the banjo. At this point I have my slots laid out and the beginnings of them cut into the nut. Look and see how far the bottoms of the slots sit above the fingerboard. As for the top edge of the nut, the strings should be half in the groove and half out, so the slots are very shallow on a finished nut. For now it is fine for them to be kind of deep. It is fine to file off the tall part of the nut a little later. I like the bottoms of the nut slots to be just a tiny bit higher than the first fret, just enough not to buzz. If you think they are close then go ahead and run a string through them and see what happens.

6. Put the bridge in place, you can measure this or just put it a little south of the middle of the head. Tune up to pitch. Are the strings hard to press down on the first fret? If so that means the action is too high from the nut. Hold the string down at the first fret. If you can see a large gap between the strings and the fingerboard at the 12th fret that means that

the bridge is too high. Take it off and trim it down. You probably don't need to release the tension from the strings to slip the bridge out, or worry about keeping the instrument in exact tune right now. After trimming slip the bridge back in and have another look.

If you have buzzes they could be caused by a variety of things. Mess around with the buzzing string. Does it buzz when noted on every fret or just some of them?

1. The nut slot could be loose. If it only buzzes when played open that could be a good indication of a loose nut slot. In this case you may be able to deepen the slot very slightly to eliminate the buzz. You might be able to fill the slot with an epoxy/bone dust mixture and saw it again slightly narrower or shallower. Or, you might prefer to make a new nut.

2. The bridge slot could be loose. If it buzzes all the time no matter where it is fretted, it could mean that there is a loose bridge slot. Or, the bridge may simply be too low. If there is a bridge slot that is too wide deepening it is a good option. If the bridge is just too short, try a taller one. I like to keep a few bridges of varying heights on hand during set up, just to experiment with. Tighten the head if it is sagging too much.

3. There could be a high fret or a low fret. If it only buzzes at one place it could be a high fret. Take a straight edge, put the thin edge against the fretboard and have a look. Are there any high or low frets? Does the straight edge rock any? If a fret is high it may have crept up after fretting. Look to see that all frets are seated properly. If a fret is not seated properly give it a little tap with the softest side of your fretting hammer. If a fret is low then you may have to remove the strings and level all the other frets down to its level, and then crown the frets again.

Intonation and Tinkering

The intonation of a fretted instrument is what makes it play in tune with itself, it depends on the placement of the bridge. To test the intonation play the string open and then play the same string fretted on the 12th fret. If the note sounds sour somehow it means that the intonation is out. An electronic tuner might come in handy for this operation. Move the bridge toward or away from the nut to adjust the intonation. Test each string until you find the spot where each note rings true. It is not uncommon for the bridge on a banjo to sit a little crooked on the head in order to play true, with the treble side being nearer the nut and the bass side being further away.

Now that the banjo is together it should be rigorously tested by playing. Whatever doesn't seem to be just right should be tinkered with. After playing and tinkering with your banjo for a while you may find that you are still not fully satisfied. In this case you should start again from the very beginning :)

Patterns, Jigs, & Forms

The **Side Profile Neck pattern** is made from thin material, like plexi-glass or thin plywood, or even cardboard. Use something that is durable. Mark a straight line that is the length of the fingerboard or use a pre-existing edge that is already straight. Then allow between 5 and 7 inches for the peghead. The peghead line should meet the first one, which represents the fingerboard, at about 7 degrees. Use a protractor to get the angle. Now make a rectangle about 3/8"-1/2" thick, this makes the peghead part of the pattern. Now go to the opposite end of the fingerboard measurement and make another straight line at 87 degrees perpendicular to the fingerboard line. This line will correspond to the intended depth of the rim, I usually go about 3". If it turns out to be too deep it can trimmed later. From the last line you marked make another line that meets it and runs parallel to the fingerboard. Measure up towards the peghead 3" or so. If you are unsure whether you will build an 11" or 12" rim be generous and the neck blank can be trimmed to size later. This makes up the heel part of the pattern. Now return to the first line, the line that represents the fingerboard, at the peghead end and measure 1" where the neck meets the back of the peghead. Now go to the heel end and measure 1 1/2" from the fingerboard line. Connect the back side of the heel box with the backside of the neck line with a gentle curve. This completes the layout of the neck pattern. Cut it out carefully.

The **Front Profile Neck Pattern** can be made from the same material as the side profile neck pattern. You can develop this pattern from a banjo or you can make it from scratch. To make it from scratch draw a straight line the length of the fingerboard. This will be the center line. You might consider marking the center line with a scratch awl if you are using plexi-glass. Decide which end of the line is to be the peghead end. I like the width of the nut to be 1 1/4" or just a little less, so mark a line 90 degrees to the center line. The center line should divide this line

Templates for the peghead, the front profile of the neck, and the side profile.

into equal halves. Now go to the other end of the center line and mark another line at 90 degrees. This line's length should be between 1 3/4" and 2", I like 2". The center line should also divide this line into equal halves. Go ahead and connect the two lines that run perpendicular to the center line on the treble side of the neck pattern. Now is the time when a fret rule comes in handy. Find where the fifth fret will be. I like my necks to be 1 5/8" wide at the fifth fret. Mark a line perpendicular to the center line at this spot. Now make a line parallel to the center line that begins at the base side of the nut line and runs down to the fifth fret line. Go to the rim end of the pattern and make another line parallel to the center line that runs from the outside of the bass side of the neck pattern up to the outside of the fifth string mark. Mark out a place for the fifth string pip to sit. Cut it out carefully. File down any rough edges.

The **Peg Head Pattern** begins with a center line. A peghead can have many shapes, the main thing is that it be able to accommodate the tuning machines. I use a quarter as a layout tool, its diameter roughly approximates the space that a tuning machine needs to be able to turn properly. The only other essential element of the peghead pattern is that it be the same width at the nut as the front profile neck pattern.

The **Neck heel dowel stick hole jig** could take a variety of forms depending on what tooling is available. The essential elements of this jig is that it be able to hold the neck blank in place while being drilled and that it hold the neck at the proper angle. A wedge shaped block can be made to hold the neck at the correct angle, about 3 degrees. The jig should accommodate clamping some how. Find a way to make sure that the drill bit will drill the hole at the correct angle. The rest of the features of this jig depend on the tool. Think it over and make some drawings if you need to.

The **Neck heel radius jig,** seen above, is used to assist in cutting the heel of the neck so that it will mate cleanly with the rim. It helps us cut an angle and a radius at the same time. It consists of a plate that screws onto the saw table of a band saw. The plate of the jig has two halves, one half has a convex arc and the other has a concave arc. The arc should have a diameter a tiny bit less than the diameter of the rim you intend to use. On the side of the plate that has the concave arc there should be a wedge that will hold the neck at 3 degrees from the plane of the plate. This jig can be made from wood or it could be made from metal as seen above. To see this jig in action refer to page 21.

The **Neck heel sanding jig** also uses a wedge to create the correct neck angle. A sanding wheel slightly smaller than the diameter of the rim may be used to remove any rough stuff on the surface of the neck heel which mates with the rim.

The **Dowel stick holding jig** simply holds the stick square to the tenon cutter. It should allow for clamping and fit whatever tool you happen to have.

The **Neck heel tension hoop rabbet jig** should represent an arc just slightly larger than the tension hoop. It should accommodate clamping and possibly allow for being held in a vise. It too should employ a wedge so that the tension hoop rabbet will mirror the angle and arc of the heel.

Strip bending spools are used to wrap the rim strips around while they are hot and while they are cooling down. I used several layers of plywood glued together to make a square about 4" thick. I then cut out a circle about 10" in diameter. These spools should have some big holes drilled in them to accommodate the use of clamps. They should also have a mouth to stick one end of the strip into to hold it while it is rolled onto the spool.

The **Rim clamping form** is made from several layers of plywood glued together like the spools. The wall of the form needs to be at least 2" thick so that it can withstand the clamping pressure. The inside diameter should be just ever so slightly larger than the intended outside diameter of the rim. The pieces that are cut out of the middle of the form can be saved for use as cauls.

Printed in Great Britain
by Amazon.co.uk, Ltd.,
Marston Gate.